There's Jews in Texas?

Winner of the 2011 Chapbook Contest
Poetica Magazine, Contemporary Jewish Writing

There's Jews in Texas?

Poems by
Debra L. Winegarten

*For my brother JD —
Kindred spirit —
you touch my heart!*

Other books by the author

Strong Family Ties:
The Tiny Hawkins Story,
with Ruthe Winegarten

Katherine Stinson:
The Flying Schoolgirl

Mum's the Word:
A Tribute to Ruthe Winegarten

Copyright © 2011 Debra L. Winegarten
All rights reserved. No part of this book may be used or reproduced in any manner whatsoever without written permission except in the case of brief quotations in critical articles and reviews. First edition.

Final Judge: Daniel Pravda Pearlman
Cover Photo: David Hoffman, Evant Texas

Book Order:
Debra Winegarten
www.sociosights.com

Published by:
Poetica Publishing Company
www.poeticapublishing.com
P.O. Box 11014
Norfolk, VA 23516

36 pages (ppb)
ISBN 978-0-9836410-6-3

To my grandparents, of blessed memory:
Celia Cohen Lewin and Charles Lewin
Louise Wollenberg Winegarten
and Samuel Winegarten

Table of Contents

Second Grade, Part One   1

Second Grade, Part Two   2

Second Grade, Part Three   4

Permission Slip, 1966   5

Passing   6

The Three R's   8

Being on Time   10

Kaddish   11

Thanksgiving   13

Swinging   14

The Price of a World   15

The Pitch Pipe   17

Hineni   18

Second Grade, Part One

In far North Dallas in the early 1960s,
At Thomas C. Gooch Elementary School
We sat in rows, alphabetically by last name.
Mark Washington in front of Debra Winegarten.

And our locker assignment came in that order, too.
So when the only Jew, Me, was assigned
A locker with the only Negro, Him,
I naturally thought

They were putting the Negro
And the Jew together
Because we had to look out for one another.
And I've been trying to do that, ever since.

Second Grade, Part Two

Being eight years old means walking
Alone to the Skillern's Drug Store
At the Park Forest Shopping Center
With my weekly allowance quarter
Searing a hole in my already-sweaty shorts pocket.

I know what I'll buy—
The latest Superman or Batman comic book
Whichever one came in that week
And doesn't already live in the pile on my nightstand at home.

With my new Superman comic slipped in the sleek paper bag
Top carefully folded so my sweaty hands don't ruin my treasure,
A grown man stops me on the sidewalk,
Eyeing my Star of David necklace and asking if I'm Jewish.

When I nod yes, (I'm not supposed to talk to strangers),
He tells me that's really too bad for me,
Because didn't I know that
Jews burn in Hell when they die?

Tears falling so hard I could barely see,
I dropped my weekly treasure and ran home
To Mom so fast I thought
I might keel over before I got to her
And be snatched right down to Hell.

When I told Mom what happened,
She put both hands on my shoulders,
Knelt to my height where she could look square in my eyes,
And in that Dallas drawl of hers, said,

"That's okay, honey, don't worry.
We're Jewish.
We don't believe in hell."

Second Grade, Part Three

"That's an A-flat," I told my music teacher.
"That's middle C," I said, when she played the next note.
"That one's easy, it's G," I said,
My back turned to the keyboard as she hit the next ivory.

"You've got perfect pitch!" she said, excitement in her voice,
And told me to stay after class.
I thought I was in trouble for knowing the notes without looking.
After class, she told me, "It's a gift from God."

"It is?" I said. "Is it because I'm Jewish?"
"You are?" asked my Catholic music teacher.
"You have a special connection to God.
You can pray to Him directly."

"You can, too," I protested,
Secretly wondering how having perfect pitch
Gave me a direct line to God.

Permission Slip, 1966

In case of an atomic bomb dropping on downtown Dallas:
_____ (a) keep my child at school and I will pick him up in my car;
_____ (b) keep my child at school until the attack is over;
_____ (c) let my child walk home.

"Ridiculous," my mother declared,
Tearing the note in tiny pieces.
"In case of an atomic attack,
We will all be dead."

I told my third-grade teacher
I lost the note.

Passing

When I was sixteen
I got to play the Voice of God
In my Sunday School confirmation play.

From there, I went on to
Impersonate doctors
On a regular basis.

Like the time at Emma Long Park
When a teenager was dragging
His distressed puppy into the water.

I marched right over and said,
"I'm a vet. Stop that right now.
You are doing serious damage to your dog."

Wearing a bathing suit,
I couldn't be expected to have my license
With me, so I passed.

Or when I had to reach the lawyer
To answer whether the medical Power of Attorney
Gave me permission to let my sister die.

I said I was a doctor just to get through
The receptionist. Now, she calls me
"Dr. Winegarten" whenever I ring them up.

The best story, of course, was my good friend,
Katherine D'Unger, who saw teenagers
Tormenting a kitten near a gas station trashcan.

Pulling her pistol out of her car's glove box,
She put it in her purse, walked over and calmly said,
"Put the cat down."

"Who are you?" one acne-faced boy sneered.
Pulling out her gun, she pointed and said,
"I'm the fucking Cat Police. Put the cat down."

They dropped the kitten and ran.

The Three R's

Someone told me once that people
Die in sets of threes
So the week Mom died
I looked to see who else went with her.

First, it was Ronald Reagan
Which really put a crimp
In the amount of newspaper coverage
Mom got.

Wasn't she the mother of Texas women's history?
Didn't she write 18 books on the subject?
Hadn't she spent her whole life telling women's stories,
Wasn't she worth at least a newspaper column?

Instead, the media followed Ronnie's casket
From one corner of the country to the other
As if all the homeless people he helped create
Would somehow want to come and pay their respects.

Ray Charles was a little easier to bear
Mom loved the blues and black men
I figure between the two of them,
They somehow balanced out Ronnie.

So the three are inextricably linked for me now
Ronnie, Ray Charles, and Ruthe.
Fitting company,
Celebrities in their own ways.

Being on Time

Three things are for certain, the sages tell us,
The time of your birth, the time of your death,
And your appearance at Judgment Day.
All the rest is negotiable.

If the time of a person's death is predetermined,
What does that say about someone committing suicide?
This act seems so selfish.
Could it be, instead, a way to keep one's appointment with God?

Kaddish

Ears strain to hear the door slam
Footsteps tread softly in the hall
That's number eight.
The chanting continues.

Three more prayers
Until *Kaddish*
Someone steps out of the chapel
Phoning to rouse an absent congregant.

The distant door slams again
Footsteps
That's number nine—
One to go.

Listening, listening, praying
For the last one
Number ten
The number needed for *minyan*.

Can't say the mourner's prayer
Until ten Jewish adults
Are in the room
Must be ten to make a *minyan*.

Is the ten person requirement
For the community—
Or is it so the group
Can keep their eyes on the grieving one?

Thanksgiving

Days before Thanksgiving
She placed scraps of torn paper on platters.

A conductor tuning her orchestra,
Sweet potato casserole here,
Cranberry sauce in crystal dish there
No detail left to chance.

Mom would call—
"I'll pay for the turkey if you'll pick it up."
I would brave the harsh Austin early morning wind
To cook the bird at her house.

Eight years have passed since we've shared
Thanksgiving dinner together.
Perhaps this year I'll set an extra place
Like Elijah at Passover, I'll open the door and invite her in.

Swinging

She sits on her porch swing.
She loved this house
And made us promise to keep her here
As long as possible.

Sweet moments with her
Were swaying together on this chained,
Dangling slatted wooden chair
Talking of life, relationships, the world.

The gnarled oak tree shadows the front porch
Its misshapen elf's face knot keeping watch on the house.
I wanted to put in a clause to protect that tree when I sold the place
So he could keep his eye on Mom's spirit.

With her death, the house sits empty.

But on a quiet, moon-dark night
When the street light burns out
If you glance out of the corner of your eye just right
You can see a shimmer of her,
Sitting on her porch swing,
 Watching, waiting, watching, waiting.

The Price of a World

If it happened in Austin
Would anyone know?
If it happened in New York City
Would anyone care?

Because it happened in Israel—
To Jews—it matters?

It happened to Jews in Itamar
Living in a West Bank settlement.
Does the illegitimacy of their place
Give throat-slitting permission?

Five people knifed to death in their home
Ruth, the mother, Rabbi Udi, her husband,
Eleven-year-old Yoav reading in bed,
Elad, the four-year old
And the three-month old baby, what did she do?

What worlds are now forever gone?
Songs unwritten, canvases blank,
The diplomacy of a country
Cut off. Silenced.

And in its place, what world arises?
Will retaliation and hatred gather
Like the waves of a tsunami
And dash to pieces all hopes of peace?

At the end of the day, we are all Fogels
A piece of my heart, ripped open,
Knifed. I know the pain of a mother murdered.
I hear her cry in the still of the night.

The Pitch Pipe

My second-grade music teacher
First discovered my hidden talent.
My back to the piano, I called out
The exact name of each note played.

"Perfect pitch, that's what you have,"
She said, in awe, to my eight-year-old face.
Devout Catholic, she asked me to pray for her
"But you can talk to God yourself," I protested.

"No, not like you can. You're special.
Jews are God's chosen people.
You have a direct channel."
Confused, I thought connecting with God had to do with perfect pitch.

One day I met a cantor-turned-Rabbi
Who, when he sang *"Adonai,"* the name of God;
For the first time, my heart cracked open and
I heard God. Right in the middle of my chest.

I found out much, much later
That the soul's job here is to get attuned to God.
I like to think of my Rabbi
As my *Yiddishe* tuning fork.

Hineni

Looking at the two almost elderly women,
I knew instantly. *Mispocheh*,
No doubt about it.

There was a certain something,
As they, time-zone fatigued,
Gathered their suitcases.

"Sisters?" I wondered,
Noting how close they stood to each other.
No, not that, they were too uncomfortable together.

But something kept drawing me to them
As if I knew them,
Maybe not from this time, but I knew them all the same.

I'm always on the lookout for Jews
It's almost an instinctual response
Like the duckling, looking for its mother.

"Are you my people?" I wondered.
But more than that was an inner knowing,
*"You **are** my people, we are from the same tribe."*

It wasn't until days later, on the Nile riverboat
When I learned their grandparents were from Grodno
Where my great grandmother was born.

Perhaps I've been reading too much Jewish mysticism lately
Learning we are reborn again and again
And there were 600,000 Jews at Mount Sinai.

Those Jews shared a revelatory moment
And perhaps, each incarnation we find each other anew
And one of us holds the memory for all.

The one woman I was drawn to instantly
Carried an air of sadness and isn't-quite-rightness
The entire first part of our journey.

Sitting together at breakfast, I asked her
How she happened to come on this trip
And why she wasn't having much fun.

Ros said her husband died two years ago this week
And her sister-in-law's husband wasn't well enough to come
And her own daughter said, "*Nu*, so what else better you have to do?"

And so she came, begrudgingly, unwillingly, alone.
"Mel would have loved this trip," she declared,
Tears bursting like the Nile from both eyes.

I talked about how sad I was after Mom died.
That for years nothing was fun and I lost my laugh.
And how afraid I was I would never find it again.

And my days of crying, slogging my way to *minyan*,
Therapy, exercise, *minyan*,
Fighting my way back from the grief underworld.

After that I made a point to spend a little time
With her each day, listening, touching,
Witnessing, reassuring her that sadness is also part of life.

Our last day together in Cairo I hired a car
And we five Jews on the tour, plus two friends
Went to the Ben Ezra synagogue.

The *shul* of Moses Maimonides, medieval philosopher.
Ros and I walked in together and stood speechless.
Turned to each other with tear-filled eyes.

"It's so beautiful," we said at the same time, in awe.
The regular caretaker had the day off, so an Egyptian man
Struggled to give us a tour.

"No pictures. No praying. Women used to be upstairs only."
"*No praying?*" I thought, "*that can't be right.
This is a synagogue, for God's sake!*"

Maybe I'd been away from *minyan* too long
But I thought, "*Who's going to be mad at me for praying -- God?*"
And marched up front and chanted the *Shema* as loud as I could.

The next thing I knew, Artie said to Mort,
"Let's say *Kaddish* for Mel, it's his *yahrzeit*."
And so we five Jews from Bus A began the prayer.

And the little Egyptian man came over and
Moved the rope barrier over so we could get closer
To the *bema*.

"*Uh oh, we don't have a minyan,*" I thought,
As the tourists around us broke into silence,
Listening to our prayer.

But our prayers got louder, not quieter,
As more voices joined in, two from Florida,
Two from Philadelphia, one from New York.

I like to think of it as the miracle of the *minyan*
There in Moses Maimonides' *shul* in Cairo, Egypt,
Where the Jews heard their own call to prayer, and answered.

Acknowledgments

I am grateful to the editors of the journals in which these poems, some in different form, first appeared.

Texas Poetry Calendar 2010 (Dos Gatos Press);
Permission Slip, 1966

Austin International Poetry Festival Anthology 2010;
The Three R's

About the Cover Photo

"It was common to have a photo made into a postcard to send home to one's family in Europe. Charles Hoffman had this picture made in Fort Worth, Texas, around 1914. He is pictured here looking at a blown-up photo of his fiance in Russia to let her know he was thinking of her. She lent him the money for his passage. However, he met another young woman in the U.S. and married her, instead."

From "Deep in the Heart, The Lives & Legends of Texas Jews," Winegarten and Schechter, Eakin Press, 1990.

Photo used with permission from David Hoffman.

About the Author

Born and raised in Dallas, Texas, Debra's poetry career began in third grade when her piece, "God is Everywhere" was published in the Temple Emanu-El newsletter. This third-generation Texan pursued degrees in sociology, first at Texas Woman's University, and The Ohio State University, where she specialized in ethnomethodology. Her first published sociological piece was a biography of the Jewish philosopher, Hannah Arendt.

After returning to Texas, she co-authored with her mother, Ruthe Winegarten, the biography of Dr. Leona "Tiny" Hawkins, one of the first African-Americans in Texas to own her own nursing home. Debra's writing career took off with her second book, "Katherine Stinson: the Flying Schoolgirl," a story of the fourth woman in the US to earn her pilot's license in 1912. This book was a finalist in Forward Magazine's young adult fiction category for Book of the Year Award.

"There's Jews in Texas?" is Debra's first poetry chapbook. When not writing poetry, she writes biographies of Texas women for middle school readers. She works at The University of Texas at Austin's Astronomy Department for the world's most supportive boss, G. Fritz Benedict. Debra lives with her heart partner, Cindy Huyser, who brings in most of the money so Debra can pursue her writing dreams. This makes her the best partner in the world. They are both owned by many cats, who supervise them closely at all times.